MAYLAND AERODROME

1928 – 1940

The story of a small independent airfield

Anthony K. Philpot

IAN HENRY PUBLICATIONS

The aircraft on the front cover is
De Havilland 84 Dragon I
G-ACAN 'Maylands'

Published by
Ian Henry Publications, Ltd
20 Park Drive, Romford, Essex RM1 4LH
and printed by
L.P.P.S. Ltd
128 Northampton Road, Wellingborough NN8 3PJ

This book is dedicated to my dear wife
Diane,

but is also dedicated
to the memory of the man who started me on this quest:

Sergeant Frederick William Boxall
of 65(F) Squadron, Hornchurch.

Without Billy's fatal accident on 25th May, 1937
research that resulted in this book
would probably never have taken place

FOREWORD

It gives me great pleasure to write this introduction to this book. Mr Anthony Philpot has brought great skill, ability and research in presenting this history. There must still be people who remember aircraft flying from this aerodrome to other places in England, also between London and Paris. The actual time involved probably compares favourably with that needed for journeys to and from Stanstead, Heathrow and Gatwick. The thrill of flying enjoyed by passengers using Maylands was much more pleasant and relaxed and the complications of reaching London after landing at Maylands, with the A12 straight and quiet, must have been much less fraught.

This land remains a beautiful reminder of the rural countryside. Major road-works only border these peaceful and picturesque acres. Before the aerodrome and before the farm, this was a Royal Hunting Forest. Now it has come full circle and the deer, free of any predators, peacefully graze the same land.

Philip S. Taylor

Since this book has been compiled, Mr Taylor has sold Maylands Golf Club to new owners. I would like to thank him him for all his assistance with this publication and to wish him all the very best in any future plans. AKP

An aerial view taken in the early 1930s before the main Hillman hangers were built. The Romford-Chelmsford Road is in the bottom right hand corner of the picture

INTRODUCTION

This book attempts to recapture the brief colourful history of Maylands farm aerodrome, and all those people that in some way have contributed to its rise to fame. Edward Hillman, without doubt, would be its biggest benefactor in this story, helping it to grow from a small privately owned landing strip to become a very successful passenger aerodrome in the early 1930s.

My own interest in this story had really started purely by accident, I suppose. At the time I was working for the London Borough of Havering Library Service which gave me excellent access to most local history, and with most of my spare time taken up as a member of the RAF Hornchurch Association, who are a local voluntary group dedicated to helping to keep the memory alive of all the men and women who had served on the fighter station during two world wars. So you can probably see how I became involved in starting this project.

The first steps into this story began when I borrowed Eric Smith's book *'First things first'*, a history of RFC Suttons Farm and RAF Hornchurch, 1915 - 1962. Under the 1937 entry he relates of a fatal crash on Maylands aerodrome that he believed had involved an aircraft from 74 'Tiger' squadron. I, like most other people, had probably only ever come across the name of Maylands Golf club, and had never seen or heard of any reference to an aerodrome. But as luck would have it I worked with someone, who, like his father, had lived in the Harold Wood area all his life, so I mentioned the incident to Jim who said that he was sure his father remembered seeing the crash site from over the boundary fence. Well, sure enough, when I interviewed Mr Nightingale he told me that he remembers seeing the local village constable standing guard over the crumpled up RAF aircraft.

My interest for more information on the crash then began to grow, as it did for tracing anything on the actual history of this long lost aerodrome. I spent many hours searching through the old newspaper files and then cross referencing it through books, looking for anything that might relate to either the accident or the aerodrome, and the more I found the more I wanted to know, my wife even said that it had almost become an obsession, and in a way I suppose it had. After all I had now started the creation of this 'monster' and I would have to see it through to its completion.

Even though it took me about eighteen months to finally lay the mystery of 1937 crash to rest, I was finally able to confirm that the accident had in fact involved a Gloster Gauntlet K 7828 of 65 (F) squadron flying from RAF Hornchurch. It was also through my intense investigative work that I was able to trace the pilot's step-brother, Mr Charles Whitby, who has been very supportive in helping me with his brother's story.

Even though the aerodrome only existed for twelve years, it had in that time established itself as the first permanent aerodrome in the county of Essex.

So from its humble beginnings in 1928 until it reached the pinnacle of its success between 1931 and 1934, that was certainly due to the reign of its proprietor Mr Edward Hillman. Although the aerodrome continued to operate successfully after his departure, it unfortunately never again reached the dizzy heights it once knew. Its demise came on the night of the 6th February 1940, when, in a blaze of glory, the whole site was burnt to the ground.

Today if you travel along either the A12 or the M25 roads that border the field the unsuspecting passerby would probably not even realise that this very unassuming piece of land held so many aviation stories from the past. All I hope is that this brief history of Maylands farm aerodrome, goes some way towards helping to keep its memory living on in our minds.

Anthony K. Philpot

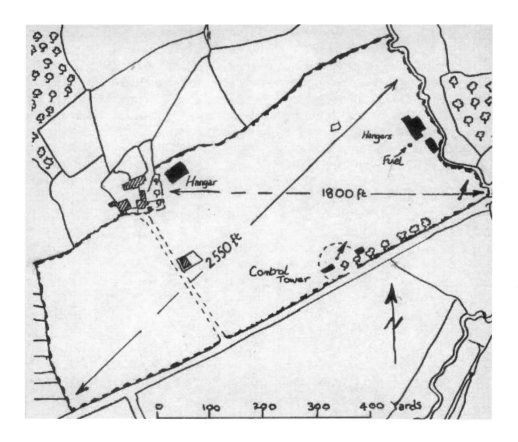

MAYLANDS AERODROME 1928-1940

When you ask most people of today's generation, 'What do you know about Maylands?' their first reaction is, 'Oh, you mean the golf course!', but how many people actually realise that it was once a thriving aerodrome of the 1930s, and that it housed the largest independent airline anywhere in the country, that of Hillman's Airways.

The site itself dates back to around 1420, when it was referred to as Mellond, but in 1772 the name Maylands seemed to have become the spelling we know it as today. The Maylands farm, the Red House and Dagnum Park Manor by 1772, had all been sold to Sir Richard Neave's family, where it remained through many generations until the 1919 land sale when it was decided by its then owner Sir Thomas Neave, to sell off the majority of the estate, keeping just a small piece of land to be passed on to his son. One of Sir Thomas's tenants at the time of the 1919 sale, was Mr G Gotheridge who had worked on the land for some years, and so he took the opportunity of buying the farm and soon the Gotheridge family farm, would become very well known for its pure milk supply diary, fresh fruits and for its superbly bred shire horses.

By 1928 one of the fields was leased out to Mr A H Matthews to be used as a private landing strip for his own Avro 504k and the four aircraft owned by the Inland Motor Services Limited. The farm's use would drastically change overnight from its agricultural use to it becoming one of the most important parts in the jigsaw of Essex aviation history.

Captain Glover's De Havilland Moth at Maylands, early 1930s

There had been almost a decade with no real flying activity throughout the county, with Maylands now being the only permanent aerodrome anywhere in Essex, as North Weald, Hainault Farm and Sutton's Farm Airfields had all closed down, although Sutton's Farm was due to reopen on the 1st April 1928, as RAF Hornchurch.

The new Maylands aerodrome had been established on the front sloping field running along the north side of the A12 trunk road, which had been the Roman road to Colchester, so the location of the aerodrome was well positioned for easy access by road or from the nearby railway station at Harold Wood. The main entrance was approximately halfway between Woodstock Avenue and the Weald Brook, just before what is now the M25 turn off. This entrance was still visible up until the early 1960s, when the Essex County Council turned the A12 into a dual carriageway.

The farm driveway once dissected the field, but today this is used as the main entrance into the Maylands Golf Club. The two original farm cottages that once stood about halfway down the drive, were so badly damaged by a German parachute mine, that they had to be demolished to make way for two post war houses.

An aerial photograph, taken on 1st February, 1998, looking north across Maylands with the drive visible in the bottom left hand corner and the A12 in the foreground

HILLMAN'S EARLY YEARS

Although over the years much has been written about Edward Hillman's notorious rise to fame, it must be said that not all that has been documented about him has been in his favour, as quotes referring to his arrogance, stubbornness and his hot blooded temper towards his workers can regularly be found, but whatever may be said of him it should certainly not be forgotten that without his shrewd business mind, dogged determination and his readiness to work hard for what he wanted, we today may not have had many of the things that we now take for granted in our air, coach and bus travel.

Edward Hillman in his daily appearance was certainly not what you might expect of a high powered travel pioneer, although not one to miss out on some free publicity stunt, he could still be found driving one of his buses or tinkering with a greasy engine in the workshop.

Edward Henry Hillman was born in Croydon in 1889, in a very humble background with most of his early years spent with very little schooling, but this did not seem to hinder young Master Hillman in any way, in fact it was probably a very good education for his later life.

By the time he reached the tender age of nine Edward was sent out to work for a local brush maker, where he stayed until aged twelve, when he made the decision to go to the nearest recruiting office to sign up with the Essex Regiment as a drummer boy, and by the time he left the army in 1918 he had risen to the rank of sergeant major in the cavalry.

An interesting story that comes from his time in the army, tells of how he lost part of his left leg in a riding accident at Mons in France. It is said that he fell from his mount and was trappped under the horse for three days before any help arrived to free him and subsequently part of his leg had to be amputated and a wooden section fitted, and so he had to be invalided out of the army with his small, but precious, gratuity payment.

He now found himself back in civvy street and quickly decided that he would need to find some work to support his wife and family; he was offered a job as a chauffeur, and after a couple of years doing this job, and accumulating a little more money, he decided he would now buy himself a car, and he began using it for taxi work around Bow and the surrounding areas. This venture soon began to pay dividends and from the proceeds of its operation and then finally its sale, Hillman was soon able to buy into another small business.

Although still involved in the transport world, he now switched his attentions into the hire, sale and repair of pedal cycles at a small shop at 52b Romford Road, Stratford. Before too long the far sighted Mr Hillman was looking at branching out into yet another new venture - the long distance motor transport business and early in 1928 with his limited resources he purchased his first bus, which he drove himself with his sixteen year old son,

His first commercial route, starting on 7th December that year, ran between Stratford and Brentwood and by the end of 1929 had been extended through Chelmsford to Colchester, which proved to be a very profitable venture. In 1930 the route was pushed on to Clacton, by when there were fifty-four departures a day from Stratford, although the timetable thinned at Brentwood, Chelmsford and Colchester.

A Hillman bus in Romford Market en route to Stratford

One of the main reasons for the success of all the routes was that Edward Hillman always seemed to be one step ahead of the other bus operators. He knew that the public wanted luxurious travel at an inexpensive price, and local fares were available all down the road. When trade was brisk he ran coaches for long-distance passengers only, reducing to all passengers using the same coach when trade was slack. He was able to do this by introducing many revolutionary measures into his fare structure and was the first bus operator to bring in both the penny fare and the season ticket.

He rapidly acquired new coaches and his fleet grew from eighteen in March, 1930, to fifty-seven by the following December. That summer the service had again expanded with six journeys a day to Ipswich, with two daily on to Great Yarmouth and two to Norwich. The single fare to Clacton and Ipswich was five shillings, Yarmouth six shillings and Norwich seven shillings and sixpence.

Early in 1931 Edward Hillman acquired a new service from Aldgate to Upminster and by 1932 he was running seventy departures a day from his new depot in Bow with fifteen minute intervals on the Brentwood run between 6.15 a.m. and 11.30 p.m.

Hillman's Upminster bus service to Upminster at the Crown, Roneo Corner. The General bus behind is also going to Upminster

Gilford JD 1229 terminating outside the *Stratford Empire* after a Chelmsford run

Hillman's Daily Service.

Head Office :— 52b and 52c Romford Road, Stratford, E. 15.

Phones : Maryland 2591—2.

I6 TIMES DAILY SERVICE

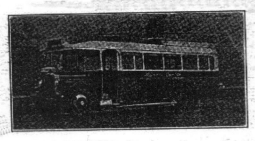

FROM

STRATFORD

TO

Romford, Brentwood,

AND

Chelmsford

FARES :	Single		Return	
	S.	D.	S.	D.
Stratford to Chelmsford	2	0	3	6
Forest Gate ,,	2	0	3	6
Manor Park ,,	1	10	3	2
Ilford ,,	1	9	3	0
Goodmayes ,,	1	9	3	0

SEASON TICKET RATES on APPLICATION

All Coaches will stop if you hail them.

ALL COACHES START FROM AND RETURN TO STRATFORD EMPIRE.

THE HADDEN PRESS, 11, Shrewsbury Road, E.7

TIME TABLE

	a.m.	a.m.	a.m.	a.m.	a.m.	a.m.	p.m.	p.m.	p.m.	p.m.	p.m.	p.m.	p.m.	p.m.	p.m.	p.m.
STRATFORD (Purdy, Broadway) ... dep.	6 0	7 30	8 0	9 0	10 0	11 30	12 15	0 2	30	3 30	4 30	5 30	6 0	7 15	8 30	9 0
STRATFORD (J. R. Roberts Stores) ..	6 0	7 30	8 0	9 0	10 0	11 30	12 15	0 2	30	3 30	4 30	5 30	6 0	7 15	8 30	9 0
FOREST GATE (Era Electrical Co.) ,,	6 5	7 35	8 5	9 5	10 5	11 35	12 20	5 2	35	3 35	4 35	5 35	6 5	7 20	8 35	9 5
MANOR PARK (Broadway) ,,	6 10	7 40	8 10	9 10	10 10	11 40	12 25	10 2	40	3 40	4 40	5 40	6 10	7 25	8 40	9 10
ILFORD (Hayden's, Ilford Hill) ,,	6 15	7 45	8 15	9 15	10 15	11 45	12 30	15 2	45	3 45	4 45	5 45	6 15	7 30	8 45	9 15
,, (Lockwood Garage, High Rd.) ,,	6 20	7 50	8 20	9 20	10 20	11 50	12 35	20 2	50	3 50	4 50	5 50	6 20	7 35	8 50	9 20
GOODMAYES (Halston, High Rd.) ,,	6 25	7 55	8 25	9 25	10 25	11 55	12 40	25 2	55	3 55	4 55	5 55	6 25	7 40	8 55	9 25
ROMFORD ,,	6 35	8 5	8 35	9 35	10 35	12 5	12 50	35 3	5	4 5	5 5	6 5	6 35	7 50	9 15	9 35
BRENTWOOD ,,	6 55	8 25	8 55	9 55	10 55	12 25	1 10	55 3	25	4 25	5 25	6 25	6 55	8 15	9 25	9 55
SHENFIELD ,,	7 0	8 30	9 0	10 0	11 0	12 30	1 15	0 3	30	4 30	5 30	6 30	7 0	8 20	9 30	10 0
MOUNTNESSING ,,	7 5	8 35	9 5	10 5	11 5	12 35	1 20	5 3	35	4 35	5 35	6 35	7 5	8 25	9 35	10 5
INGATESTONE ,,	7 10	8 40	9 10	10 10	11 10	12 40	1 25	10 3	40	4 40	5 40	6 40	7 10	8 30	9 40	10 10
MARGARETTING ,,	7 20	8 50	9 20	10 20	11 20	12 50	1 35	20 3	50	4 50	5 50	6 50	7 20	8 35	9 50	10 20
CHELMSFORD ... arr.	7 25	9 0	9 30	10 30	11 30	1 0	1 45	30 4	0	5 0	6 0	7 0	7 30	8 45	10 0	10 30

UP

	a.m.	a.m.	a.m.	a.m.	noon	p.m.	p.m.	p.m.	p.m.	p.m.	p.m.	p.m.	p.m.	p.m.	p.m.	p.m.
CHELMSFORD ... dep.	7 45	9 25	10 0	10 45	12 0	1 15	2 0	2 45	4 15	5 30	6 30	7 10	8 0	9 0	10 15	10 35
MARGARETTING ,,	7 55	9 35	10 10	10 55	12 10	1 25	2 10	2 55	4 25	5 40	6 40	7 20	8 10	9 10	10 25	10 45
INGATESTONE ,,	8 5	9 45	10 20	11 5	12 20	1 35	2 20	3 5	4 35	5 50	6 50	7 30	8 20	9 20	10 35	10 55
MOUNTNESSING ,,	8 10	9 50	10 25	11 10	12 25	1 40	2 25	3 10	4 40	5 55	6 55	7 35	8 25	9 25	10 40	11 0
SHENFIELD ,,	8 15	9 55	10 30	11 15	12 30	1 45	2 30	3 15	4 45	6 0	7 0	7 40	8 30	9 30	10 50	11 5
BRENTWOOD ,,	8 20	10 0	10 35	11 20	12 35	1 50	2 35	3 20	4 50	6 5	7 5	7 45	8 35	9 35	10 55	11 10
ROMFORD ,,	8 40	10 20	10 55	11 40	12 55	2 10	2 55	3 40	5 10	6 25	7 25	8 5	8 55	9 55	11 10	11 30
GOODMAYES (Halston, High Rd.) ,,	8 50	10 30	11 5	11 50	1 5	2 20	3 5	3 50	5 20	6 35	7 35	8 15	9 5	10 5	11 20	11 40
ILFORD (Lockwood Gar. High Rd.) ,,	8 55	10 35	11 10	11 55	1 10	2 25	3 10	3 55	5 25	6 40	7 40	8 20	9 10	10 10	11 25	11 45
,, (Hayden, Ilford Hill) ,,	9 0	10 40	11 15	12 0	1 15	2 30	3 15	4 0	5 30	6 45	7 45	8 25	9 15	10 15	11 30	11 50
MANOR PARK (Broadway) ,,	9 5	10 45	11 20	12 5	1 20	2 35	3 20	4 5	5 35	6 50	7 50	8 30	9 20	10 20	11 35	11 55
FOREST GATE (Era Electrical Co.) ,,	9 10	10 50	11 25	12 10	1 25	2 40	3 25	4 10	5 40	6 55	7 55	8 35	9 25	10 25	11 40	12 0
STRATFORD (J. R. Roberts Stores) ..	9 15	10 55	11 30	12 15	1 30	2 45	3 30	4 15	5 45	7 0	8 0	8 40	9 30	10 30	11 45	12 5
STRATFORD (Purdy, Broadway) arr.	9 15	10 55	11 30	12 15	1 30	2 45	3 30	4 15	5 45	7 0	8 0	8 40	9 30	10 30	11 45	12 5

ORDINARY BUS FARES ON THIS COACH.   P.T.O.

Sole Chelmsford Agent :- **Mr. J. PEACHEY, Confectioner, London Road Corner, Chelmsford.**   Phone — Chelmsford 82?

Hillman's business brain now went into action again when he saw the chance of entering the newly emerging world of air taxi and charter work and took his first tentative steps into the aviation scene by purchasing two Puss Moths from Brian Lewis & Company, De Havilland distributors.

It was certainly the right time to be entering the world of commercial aviation, as during the early part of the 1930s, small intrepid aviation enterprises began to spring up all around the countryside, offering exciting thrills of aerobatic displays, as well as short pleasure flights for those who could afford it and for those with the nerve to take to the air.

Many of these companies had managed to survive the great post-war slump and were now becoming very active in this newly flourishing business of pleasure flights, as well as there being many middle class people wanting to try to impress their friends by arriving at their destination by air taxi. The most prosperous of these small operators was the Brooklands School of Flying, the proud owners of two Avro 548s and boasting that they could land in almost any size field.

It wasn't until 26th November, 1931 that Mr Hillman, now owner of Hillman Saloon Coaches and Airways, Ltd., decided to take over the licence of Maylands aerodrome from its former licensee Mr A H Matthews: this was to be the start of even greater things for both Hillman's and his newly acquired Maylands.

'Gilford', Number 4 in Hillman's fleet of aircraft

The expansion to the site had started soon after Mr Hillman took over the licence, its first major improvements began on the south-east side with the filling in of ditches and the felling of some trees, to make it easier for the installation of the hangers. Edward Hillman had employed the services of Boulton & Paul to erect the buildings he needed on site, which included a control office, passenger reception area, booking office, and restaurant, plus three large hangers with workshops, the largest of the hangers measuring 100 feet square. Later, a customs office would be added.

Four principal figures in Maylands' history:
(l to r) T W Morton, Harold 'Timber' Woods, Ernest Hillman, and R D Crundall

10

Below is an extract from an article published in the October 1933 issue of *Airways and Airports magazine* entitled 'An Essex Airport'. It listed all the details and facilities which the new aerodrome would have.

Maylands Aerodrome (Romford) Essex, TQS60924.
Class -A- private licenced civil aerodrome for use only by the licensee and individuals specifically authorised - them.
Location: In the county of Essex, 3¾ miles North-East of Romford, 2¼ miles South-West of Brentwood, and on the North side of the main A12 road, in undulating wooded and generally cultitivated country with small fields, bordered - hedges.
Description: The surface is grass covered with a slight general slope to the East, the aerodrome is 130 feet above sea level. The dimensions of the landing areas are: North-South 440 yards, North-East, South-West 700 yards, East-West 600 yards, South-East, North-West 400 yards. On the North-East side there is a hedge 3 feet high, and a hanger 35 feet high; there is also a wood with trees 60 feet high, this is about 30 yards from the boundary. On the South-East side telegraph wires 25 feet high run along the side of the main road, on the South-West side there is a hedge is 3 feet high, while on the North-West side the hedge is 4 feet high, there are also farm buildings, a hanger and trees, of which the maximum height is 60 feet.
Markings and signals: - (Markings): The name Hillman is marked in white near the centre of the aerodrome. Signals (by day): Two wind sleeves are flown from masts, one is situated at the South-East corner and the other near the South-East boundary of the aerodrome. (by night): No signals. markings, or wind indicators can be used.

The hanger in August,1932, with DH Fox Moth G-ABVI just visible

Aircraft accommodation: There are three hangers in total, one 30 feet x 90 feet, one 100 feet x 100 feet and one 40 feet x 60 feet, there are also two workshops, 35 feet x 35 feet on the side of the larger hanger.

Services: All repairs can be undertaken at the aerodrome, where ground engineers are in attendance, refuelling pumps are installed, there is also a landing party available, hotel accommodation can be found at nearby Harold Wood and Brentwood. There is a railway station just 1½ miles away at Harold Wood, and a bus service to and from London, which runs past the aerodrome.

Local Regulations: Flying hours are between sunrise and sunset, charges were by arrangement with the controlling authority.

Controlling authority and licensee: Mr Edward H Hillman Esq., London Road, Romford, Essex.

Edward Hillman at Maylands with DH Puss Moth 'Gilford'

After a short period in the air charter business it became quite clear that Hillman's company would need to expand yet again, and so by the April of 1932 Hillman Airways had opened a scheduled service from Mayland to Alton Park, another small airfield on the outskirts of Clacton. He could now build upon his initial success and also be one step in front of his rivals by being the first operator to carry more of the day trippers and the holiday makers with his bus and/or services. Many families could now travel on his buses, while he could also cater for those passengers needing to reach their destination faster with his air taxi service. The journey time by air was estimated to be around thirty minutes compared to the three hours by road, and with a single air fare of just 12 shillings and sixpence (around 62 pence in pence in today's money) or a return of £1.   This fare structure also gave Hillman the upper hand over his competitors because he knew none of them would he able to undercut his prices.

BOW —CLACTON-ON-SEA SERVICE.

DOWN

	a.m.	p.m.	pm
BOW COACHING STATION ... dep.	9 0	2 15	7 0
STRATFORD (Hillman's Wtg. Rm.) „	9 5	2 20	7 5
FOREST GATE ... ... „	9 10	2 25	7 10
MANOR PARK (Broadway) ... „	9 15	2 30	7 15
ILFORD (Hayden's, Ilford Hill) ... „	9 20	2 35	7 20
„ (Lockwood Garage, High Rd.) „	9 22	2 37	7 22
GOODMAYES (Halston, High Rd.) „	9 25	2 40	7 25
ROMFORD (Hillman's Offices) „	9 35	2 50	7 35
BRENTWOOD (Yorkshire Grey) „	9 55	3 10	7 55
CHELMSFORD (London Rd. Corner, Peacher's) „	10 25	3 40	8 25
WITHAM (King's) ... ... „	11 10	4 25	9 10
COLCHESTER (Bus Park) ... „	11 45	4 50	9 35
CLACTON-ON-SEA, Hillman's Station arr.	12 30	5 45	10 30

UP

	a.m.	pm	p.m.
CLACTON-ON-SEA, Hillman's Station dep.	7 0	2 30	7 30
COLCHESTER (Bus Park) ... „	7 45	3 15	8 S 15
WITHAM (King's) ... ... „	8 25	3 50	8 55
CHELMSFORD (London Rd. Corner, Peacher's) „	9 10	4 35	9 40
BRENTWOOD (Yorkshire Grey) „	9 40	5 5	10 10
ROMFORD (Hillman's Offices) ... „	10 0	5 25	10 30
GOODMAYES (Halston, High Rd.) „	10 5	5 30	10 35
ILFORD (Lockwood Gar'ge,High Rd. „	10 8	5 33	10 38
„ (Hayden, Ilford Hill) ... „	10 10	5 35	10 40
MANOR PARK (Broadway) ... „	10 15	5 40	10 45
FOREST GATE ... ... „	10 20	5 45	10 50
STRATFORD (Hillman's Wtg. Rm.) „	10 25	5 50	10 55
BOW COACHING STATION ... arr.	10 30	5 55	11 0

S. 8.20 on Sundays only.

Our Starting Point from Clacton is HILLMAN'S COACH STATION, 125, Old Road, 100 yards on left hand side from "Warwick Castle Hotel."

REMEMBER that you can also charter an Aeroplane from us at 3d. per mile.

By June that year, the Clacton service had increased its operating time, which meant that it would now need to purchase more economical aircraft to be able to meet the growing demand from the paying public, and again Hillman Airways stayed with the tried and trusted De Havilland Aircraft Company, this time buying a DH 60m Moth to replace one of the smaller DH Fox Moths which was to be sold to Eastern Air Transport of Skegness. This initial success for Maylands as a commercial aerodrome was without doubt down to the very wise Mr Edward Hillman.

HILLMAN'S
SALOON COACHES AND AIRWAYS.

(Proprietor, E. Hillman)

Head Office:

BOW COACHING STATION, 133, BOW ROAD, E.3.

Phone : East 7101 (4 Lines).

ROMFORD :	STRATFORD :	BOW :	ILFORD :
London Road.	52b, Romford Road.	58, Bow Road.	23, High Road.
Tel. Romford 705.	Tel. Maryland 4682-3.	Tel. East 7070.	Tel. Ilford 2247.

AERODROME—Phone ROMFORD 1700   CLACTON—Phone CLACTON 62

Aerial Trips Daily

From 8 a.m. till Dusk,

AT

Hillman's Aerodrome

Mayland's Estate, ROMFORD.

For Air Rates, see other side.

FREE ADMISSION TO CAR PARK, AERODROME AND BUFFET!

Meet your Friends and watch the Flying over a Cup of Tea.

All Refreshments at Popular Prices.

Drive your car on to the Ground where it will be safe whilst you are taking Refreshments or in the Air, or travel by our Coaches direct to the Ground.

Please do not obstruct other road users by Parking your Car outside the Ground.

The Madden Press, 11, Shrewsbury Road, Forest Gate, E.7.

15

The following extract is from the *Clacton Gazette* dated 19th March, 1932 –

From Good Friday onwards Clacton will be connected by air to all parts of the British Isles and the Continent, because on Tuesday Mr E Hillman, the well known motor coach proprietor, arrived at Alton Park flying ground, Clacton, in a De Havilland Gypsy 3 Puss Moth to complete the final arrangements for the service, he later left with Mr Woods, the pilot, for Romford.

We are officially informed that a taxi hire service has been inaugurated so that those desirous of travelling by air will be able to leave Clacton at any time daily, for any destination they might require. In the very near future it is anticipated a regular daily service will operate between London, Colchester and Clacton to a scheduled timetable.

This service will be one of many to include Ipswich, Lowestoft, Yarmouth and Norwich. The journey from London to Clacton or vice versa takes twenty-five minutes. The London aerodrome is at Romford, where a taxi service to and from Clacton will consist of the famous De Havilland Gypsy 3 Puss Moth machines, the latest type for luxury travel in safety and comfort, these aeroplanes have accommodation for a pilot and two passengers.

Posing on Clacton Pier, this group of air trippers are Messrs A Grimsey, R W Fenton, E A Griffiths, and F Ross

17

Three Hillman DH Puss Moths G-ABVX, G-ABSO, and G-ABSB en route
from Alton Park, Clacton to Maylands

HILLMAN'S
SALOON COACHES
AND AIRWAYS

HEAD OFFICE · LONDON RD., ROMFORD
Phone Romford 1705 (2 lines)
Clacton Office · HILLMAN'S KIOSK, 125 OLD ROAD
Phone Clacton 62.
Aerodrome · ALTON PARK, CLACTON-ON-SEA
Phone Clacton 62.

AERIAL FLIGHTS
——— DAILY ———

9 a.m. TILL DUSK   Popular Trips at 5/-, 10/-, £1
First-class Comfort, First-class Pilots, First-class Planes

A Plane at Clacton Aerodrome.

The Clacton Aerodrome is situated from Warwick Castle
Hotel down St. Osyth Road, then first turning on left.

With the growth of the Clacton service now progressing so rapidly, Hillman had seen the potential for even greater expansion into the air taxi service and so was spurred on to stage an event that had never been seen in the county before – 'The Great Essex Air Pageant'.

This was the biggest opportunity he had ever had to get free publicity for his company and so could not afford to miss this chance to bring even more notoriety to himself and also to his expanding business empire. The spectacle would take place on 24th September, 1932, and, because Hillman's name was now widely known throughout aviation circles, he was able to persuade many prominent figures of the day to attend, probably none more prestigious than the Lord Mayor of London, Sir Maurice Jenks.

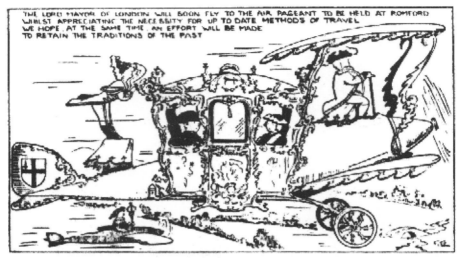

How the *Daily Mirror* saw the trip

This was another first for Edward Hillman, as he was to fly the Lord Mayor and his party down from Heston aerodrome, making Sir Maurice the first Lord Mayor of London to fly to an event.

The party of distinguished guests was flown to Maylands in a Spartan Cruiser piloted by Lieutenant Colonel L A Strange, with the Sheriffs of the county arriving in a Westland Wessex. Both aircraft were escorted by eight Wapitis of 600 City of London Squadron and three Bristol Bulldogs of 54 Squadron from nearby RAF Hornchurch.

A massive crowd of around 2,000 turned out to witness this once-in-a-lifetime

spectacular which included the Lord Mayor being introduced to pilots of 600 Squadron (on the left). One of the many highlights of the day was the air race for the Hillman Trophy, which was won by De Havilland's Hugh Buckingham, piloting a DH Fox Moth.

After the overwhelming success of the 'Air Pageant', Hillman now saw his chance to build on another idea he had been working on, that of introducing a cheap cross-channel air service, taking in Ostend, Le Bourget and Paris. The new route would only be able to operate successfully if the company invested in a more economical aircraft. A myth that grew from the need for this new aircraft was that Edward Hillman flew to

Geoffrey De Havilland's office at Stag Lane and banged a rough sketch of this twin engined plane on his desk. The truth is more likely to be that Hillman's idea was merged with De Havilland's original plans that were already underway on the drawing board – from this was born the DH 84 Dragon.

The prototype was given a test flight down to Maylands on 12th December, 1932 and was flown directly from the Stag Lane factory by De Havilland's chief test pilot, Hubert Broad. It then returned to the factory for further testing before its delivery to Hillman Airways on 20th December for its official naming ceremony. It was to be called 'Maylands' and again Hillman persuaded the 'Queen of the Air', Amy Mollison (née Johnson) to perform the task; the following year her associations with the aerodrome would continue for a short time when she took up with Hillman Airways as a pilot.

January of 1933 saw 'Maylands G-ACAN' quickly pressed into service to convey a party of Ramsgate Town Council officials between Maylands aerodrome and Manston in Kent, as a preview of the opening of his Thanet service.

The interior of G-ACAN on a test flight. Notice the utility-type seats and the narrow gangway. For its day it was the height of luxury!

G-ACAN arriving at Maylands on 20th December, 1932.
In the foreground is DH 60m Moth G-ABCW

This is a copy of the memorandum of agreement, dated 30th March, 1933, for the proposed opening of the new route between Maylands and Manston -

Memorandum of agreement made this Thirtieth March 1933 between Thanet Aviation Limited of 3 Chapel Place, Ramsgate in the county of Kent (herein called 'The Landlords' of the one part and Edward Henry Hillman, proprietor of Hillman's Airways, of London Road, Romford, in the county of Essex (herein called 'The Tenant') of the other part, whereby the Landlords agree to let and the tenants agree to hire for the term of one year from the 30th day of March, 1933, all that piece or parcel of land at Cheeseman's Farm, Manston, in the county of Kent, licensed as an aerodrome by the Air Ministry.
Yielding and by paying therefor the rent of one hundred and sixty pounds as follows:-
The sum of £40 to be paid on the signing of this agreement, the sum of £40 on the first day of June, 1933, and the sum of £80 on the 15th September, 1933.
The tenant agrees to pay the rent as the same shall become due, and to use the land as a flying ground only and not to sublet or part with the possession therefor without first obtaining the Landlord's consent in writing.
It is hereby agreed that the said rent shall also include the use of the ground known as 'Nethercourt Aerodrome' without further payment being made thereof otherwise that in respect of the two special occasions when aviation displays shall be held.
It is hereby agreed that the said Landlords shall act as booking agents for the said tenant in Ramsgate, Margate, Broadstairs and all adjacent and intermediate towns, and in consideration thereof the said Landlords shall receive a commission of 15% upon all bookings made by them. Further, in consideration of the said Landlords undertaking the sole responsibility of all bookings in respect of 'Joy Flight' from Nethercourt Aerodrome, they shall receive a commission of 25% upon all such 'Joy Rides' bookings by them.

Amy Mollison christens Hillman Airways first DH84 Dragon 1 'Maylands'
on 20th December, 1932

HILLMAN'S AIRWAYS

MAYLANDS AERODROME.

'Phone : ROMFORD '700.

LONDON — PARIS SERVICE.

London	TWICE DAILY.	Paris
10. 0 a.m.		10. 0 a.m.
13.45 p.m.		13.45 p.m.

Single fare - £3 10 0   Period return fare - £5 10 0

Special week-end, Friday to Tuesday - £4 15 0

FOREIGN FLIGHTS

This publicity shot was taken in early 1933 for the launch of the newly-opened London to Paris route. Left to right are Captain Hubert Broad (De Havilland's chief test pilot, Mrs Broad, Miss Doreen Hillman, Edward Hillman, Mr William Courtenay (*Evening Standard* Aviation reporter) and Edward Arthur John 'Sonny' Hillman

The first scheduled Hillman Airways passenger service to fly to Paris began in April, 1933; its fare structure still showed that Hillman meant business. He had once again thrown down the gauntlet to all his competitors - cutting his prices to the bare minimum with a single fare set at £3.10.0d and a return fare of £5.10.0d; he had even come up with a special weekend return fare of £5.15.0d.

A driver and his conductor pose for a picture in front of two Hillman buses outside the Bow coach station in 1931

As the year went on it was becoming more noticeable that the bus side of the business was running into trouble with the London Passenger Transport Board (LTPB), who had been pursuing the unscrupulous Mr Hillman's company over many months, trying to acquire many of his routes. It became expedient that Hillman's coaches and aircraft should part company, which they did by the end of that year. In January 1934 the LPTB had taken over, not only the majority of Hillman's bus fleet including his Upminster route and more than half his activities London to Colchester, but also the garage in London Road, Romford.

Hillman's Garage in Cotleigh Road, Romford, in 1934

The same garage two years later

The site in 2003

Edward Hillman went on to sell the rest of the bus operation, his Bow depot and twenty-eight vehicles to Eastern National. When it reached its largest number Hillman's bus operation had boasted one hundred and thirteen coaches – not bad in six years!

By August, 1934, Hillman's former bus business had been reduced to a Bow-Chelmsford route, with no local fares between Bow and Brentwood, and he could now concentrate mainly on his airline venture. Unfortunately even more disastrous news was to arrive on Mr Hillman's desk; this time it did not affect his operations on the aerodrome, but it had now been recommended that the site become an officially licensed customs aerodrome. Although this did not in itself present many problems, it was the covering note at the foot of the letter that really did the damage – 'It should be noted by the licensee Mr E H Hillman of the Romford (Maylands Farm) airport, that this site should now only be used by a restricted size of aircraft as allowed by the airport authorities.' This was the first published indication that Hillman Airways might soon have to quit the aerodrome, particularly as the new larger DH89 Dragon Rapide was due to enter service.

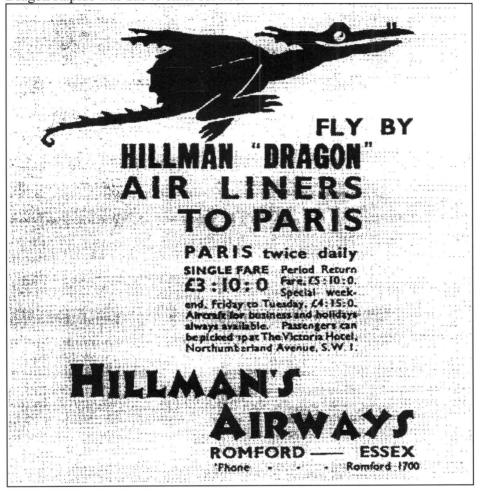

FLY BY
HILLMAN "DRAGON"
AIR LINERS
TO PARIS

PARIS twice daily

SINGLE FARE Period Return
£3:10:0 Fare: £5:10:0.
Special week-
end, Friday to Tuesday, £4:15:0.
Aircraft for business and holidays
always available. Passengers can
be picked up at The Victoria Hotel,
Northumberland Avenue, S.W.1.

HILLMAN'S
AIRWAYS
ROMFORD —— ESSEX
'Phone ·   · Romford 1700

Mr Hillman had not been idle in his efforts to build up his growing empire, because, even before the new aircraft regulations had arrived in his office, he had been negotiating to buy 180 acres of farmland at Stapleford Tawney, although his move was to come about much sooner than he had expected. Edward Hillman also had the foresight to see that he needed to have his workers close to this more isolated site and he accomplished this by having a row of twelve cottages built in Ongar Road, Abridge. On 23rd June, 1934, the Essex Airport opened for business.

Two of Hillman's buses that took passengers from his London pick-ups to the aerodrome

After Hillman's departure from Maylands, the aerodrome began slowly to revert back to being used as just another small joy riding airfield, with probably its busiest time still being at the weekends or when the flying circus displays hit town. These displays were usually performed by the Alan Cobham Flying Circus, which was the best known air display team around in the 'thirties.

This *News Chronicle* photograph shows some of the first passengers to purchase their tickets for the Paris trip

Avion de HEVILLAND de la C¹ᵉ
HILLMANS-AIRWAYS N° 1... Paris-Londres.

On French soil DH 84 Dragon I of Hillman's Airways awaits passengers for the return
flight to England

Hillman's Airways, LTD.

HEAD OFFICE:

ESSEX AIRPORT,

Stapleford, near Abridge, Essex.

Telephone—Stapleford 291 (10 lines)

Open Day and Night.

The Essex Airport is situated on the main road between Abridge and Passingford Bridge, and is a forty minute run by road from King's Cross.

All Hotel facilities are available at the Airport, and our own Express Coach Service operates between King's Cross Coaching Station and the Airport in connection with the arrival and departure of all Air Liners.

The Fares for persons wishing to travel by our Coach Service to see their friends arrive or depart, or for the purpose of visiting the Airport, are 1/6 Single; 2/6 Return.

Private Charters are carried out from 5/- upwards, and Machines are available day or night.

The Essex Airport has fully-equipped workshops, and private owners can have their machines cleaned, housed or repaired at any time of the day or night, and complete C. of A's are undertaken. A free Car Park is also provided.

In order to avoid delay passengers passing through Customs are requested not to leave the Customs Office until all the necessary formalities have been completed.

LONDON — PARIS

WINTER TIME TABLE,
UNTIL FURTHER NOTICE.

LONDON TO PARIS.

				p.m.
King's Cross Coaching Station	dep.	9 0	12 45
Essex Airport	„	10 0	1 45
Le Bourget Airport	arr.	12 0	3 45
Paris. 25, Rue Royale	„	12 30	4 30

PARIS TO LONDON.

		a.m.	p.m.
Paris, 25, Rue Royale	dep.	9 15	1 0
Le Bourget Airport	„	10 0	1 45
Essex Airport	arr.	12 0	3 45
King's Cross Coaching Station	„	1 0	4 45

FARES.

Single	Week-end Return
£3 10 0	£4 15 0

Day Return	Period Return
£4 5 0	£5 10 0

NO PASSPORTS are required for Day and Week-End Tickets. Week-End Tickets are available from Friday to the following Tuesday or any day in between.

There is no limit to the availability of Period Return Tickets but holders of open date tickets must give 24 hours notice to the Head Office in London or Paris when they wish to return.

33 lbs. of baggage is carried free of charge for each passenger, subject to the permissible load of the Air Liner not being exceeded, and baggage in excess of this weight is charged at the rate of 3d. per lb.

PARIS OFFICE:—Air Express, 25, Rue Royale.
Telephone—Anjou 14—45.

LONDON, LIVERPOOL, BELFAST, GLASGOW.

DAILY EXCEPT SUNDAYS.

ROAD TRANSPORT CONNECTIONS.

LONDON TO GLASGOW.

London		
Essex Airport	dep. 10.0 a.m.	
Liverpool		
Speke Airport	dep. 11.20 a.m.	
Belfast		
Newtownards	dep. 12.35 p.m.	
Glasgow		
Renfrew Airport	arr. 1.35 p.m.	

GLASGOW TO LONDON.

Glasgow		
Renfrew Airport	dep. 8.30 a.m.	
Belfast		
Newtownards	dep. 9.30 a.m.	
Liverpool		
Speke Airport	dep. 10.45 a.m.	
London		
Essex Airport	arr. 12.5 p.m.	

ROAD TRANSPORT CONNECTIONS.

G.P.O. Sorting Office, Victoria Street	...	dep. 10.0 a.m.
Grand Central Hotel, 18 Royal Avenue	...	dep. 12.35 p.m.
381 Argyle Street	...	arr. 1.35 p.m.

Grand Central Hotel, 18 Royal Avenue	...	11.40 a.m.
G.P.O. Sorting Office, Victoria Street	...	1.5 p.m.
Kings Cross Coaching Station	...	2.5 p.m.

Grand Central Hotel, 18 Royal Avenue	...	10.0 a.m.
G.P.O. Sorting Office, Victoria Street	...	11.5 a.m.
Kings Cross Coaching Station	...	12.5 a.m.

ROAD TRANSPORT CONNECTIONS.

Kings Cross Coaching Station	...	9.0 a.m.
G.P.O. Sorting Office, Victoria Street	...	11.0 a.m.
Grand Central Hotel, 18 Royal Avenue	...	12.5 p.m.
381 Argyle Street	...	8.0 a.m.

FARES.

	Single	Return	Excess Baggage Rate
London and Liverpool	£3 0 0	£4 5 0	6d. lb.
London and Belfast	£8 0 0	£8 0 0	9d. lb.
London and Glasgow	£6 0 0	£10 0 0	12d. lb.
Liverpool and Belfast	£4 0 0	£4 0 0	6d. lb.
Liverpool and Glasgow	£3 5 0	£5 10 0	9d. lb.
Belfast and Glasgow	£2 5 0	£3 5 0	6d. lb.

Freight carried at same rate as excess baggage with a minimum charge of 2/-.

Children under 14 years of age, two thirds of above fares.

Children under 3½ lbs. of baggage is carried free of charge for each passenger, subject to the permissible load of the Air Liner not being exceeded, but no free baggage is carried for children travelling at reduced fares.

The new licensee of Maylands was the Romford Flying Club, accompanied by the Drone Flying Club and their solitary BAC Drone aircraft. A third partner in the Maylands venture was the renowned Essex Aero, Limited, owned by Mr Jack Cross, the former Chief Engineer of Hillman's; his company would later move on to greater things at Gravesend Airport.

The whole country was now beginning to see a rise in the number of similar small independent aircraft manufacturers; one such company, based at Maylands from 1936 to 1939 was Premier Aircraft Constructions Limited, who were responsible for building the attractive Gordon Doves.

Two air-mail envelopes flown from Stapleford Tawney by Hillman's Airways

THE END OF HILLMAN'S AIRWAYS

Meanwhile, things had started fairly well for Hillman's at their new home at Stapleford (or the Essex Airport, as it more grandly called). They had already gained a new route flying to Liverpool, the Isle of Man and Belfast; soon they were rewarded with the General Post Office air mail contract, which meant that they could now add Glasgow to the original routes.

The good fortune did not last for too long, as on 2nd October, 1934 the first loss of a Hillman airliner was recorded when an 89 Dragon Rapide, G-ACPM, crashed into the sea four miles off the coast at Folkestone with the loss of the pilot, W R Bannister, and all six passengers. An official statement was issued by the Air Ministry, stating that the disaster had been put down to a lack of navigational skills by the pilot.

Even greater sadness followed this tragedy, when just two months later, on 31st December, the sudden death of Edward Hillman was announced; he was only forty-five years old.

Now, with the loss of Hillman Airways' backbone, things started to go from bad to worse and, on 21st February another tragic incident occurred, when two sisters jumped from one of Hillman Airways' aircraft over Upminster, while en route to Paris. Jane and Elizabeth Du Bois (20 and 23 respectively) were the daughters of the American Consul-General to Naples. They leapt in a lovers' pact after receiving the sad news of their fiancés' deaths in an RAF flying boat incident.

In September that year, plans were being drawn up for a merger with United Airways and Spartan Airlines and by the end of that month a new company was born, registered as Allied British Airways. Less than a month later, the name had been shortened to simply British Airways.

So, after four long, hard years of work by Edward Hillman, catapulting his name to the forefront of the business world, it had taken just nine months to end it and Hillman Airways, once a thriving independent airline, now ceased to exist.

DEVELOPMENTS AT MAYLANDS

Things went fairly quietly, as a whole, for a couple of years, but Maylands suddenly found itself back in the headlines when part of the western boundary was put up for sale to Ingrebourne Estates for the development of a golf course, which was officially opened on Saturday, 18th July, 1936.

Initially the plan was to create a public course on privately owned land, but within its first year it was decided that the course would be for private members only.

This article is from the *Romford Recorder* of 19th May, 1937

CORONATION AIR WEEK

Rain is not only bad for street teas, but it also threw a decided damper on arrangements for the start of an air week at the Maylands aerodrome, in Harold Wood. The first national aviation club had prepared for five days of aerobatic displays, pleasure trips and a fun fair, but although everything was in readiness on Coronation Day, the wet weather caused an abandonment of most of the programme.

The air week was declared open as arranged by Captain J Tunstall, M.C, J.P, but the crowning of the air queen, Miss Sylvia Burroughs, who appeared with her maids of honour, Miss Boardman and Miss Helen Masson, was put off until the weather showed signs of recovering.

Although the air displays were called off, the club officials and their friends assembled at the aerodrome for the evening dance. Thursday was to be children's day, but the state of the ground made it inadvisable to try to carry on the arrangements.

There will be an official opening today (Saturday) by Councillor C H Allen J.P. and this is to be followed by a formation flight over Romford and Brentwood. The week closes on Sunday, when there will be a session of passenger flights, competitions etc., concluded by the presentation of the prizes by the Air Queen.

This extract is from the *Romford Recorder* of Friday 8th October, 1937

GRACIE SINGS TO ROMFORD'S CHARTER MAYOR
HAS ONE AMBITION – TO LEARN TO FLY

Gracie Fields, the famous stage and screen star, has one ambition – to learn to fly.

She announced this at Maylands Flying Club, Romford, on Sunday afternoon, when she paid a visit there on behalf of her own orphanage.

Wearing a smart black ensemble, Gracie stepped from her car and was mobbed by hundreds of people, many of whom broke through the barrier to secure her autograph.

The ever-smiling, joking Gracie obliged.

She was met by the Charter Mayor and Mayoress of Romford (Mr and Mrs C H Allen) and Captain R Gordon.

On his address of welcome the Charter Mayor said many nice things about the star, "You are loved by all, Gracie!" was one of the compliments her paid her (feigned embarrassment from Gracie).

"What about a song?" shouted the crowd after the welcome.

"Aw reet, I'll make a bit of noise," said Gracie. "What would you like?"

"Sweethearts" and "Sally" came the reply. So Gracie sang.

In the middle of the song 'Sweethearts' she remarked, "I am singing this for the Mayor," winking her eye at the crowd.

She then sang 'Sally' and the crowd joined in the chorus. "Louder," said Gracie, "just imagine you're in our front room having a bit of a sing-song."

A bouquet was presented to her by Miss June Gordon.

The star was entertained to tea at the Maylands Golf Club by members.

As a vice-president of the club, the Charter Mayor welcomed her. He spoke of the excellent work she was doing. "You are not only putting yourself at the top of the ladder, you are doing so much good for the rest of humanity, and we all love you for it," he said.

Gracie replied saying that God had been very good to her. She had always tried to do unto others as she had been done by.

As she was about to sit down she eyed the assortment of food, saying, "Now we are going to get something for 'nowt. I didn't think I was coming to such a 'do'."

At tea she was handed a basket of flowers by Mrs Hobday (lady captain of the club).

The Charter Mayor announced that £50 had already been sent from the district to the Gracie Fields' Orphanage. All the proceed that day were in aid of her orphanage.

After Miss Fields' departure, a number of her songs and gramophone records were auctioned and realised a useful sum towards charity. Mr H D Cowan was the auctioneer. Later in the evening Miss Gladys Ripley, the B B C artiste, visited the club and was persuaded to sing. This started an impromptu concert, which continued until the end of the evening.

A FLYING FATALITY

During its brief life as an aerodrome, Maylands saw quite a few flying accidents and on 25th May, 1937, it was to witness yet another – that of the tragic loss of a young serving RAF pilot recently attached to 65 (F) Squadron, based at the nearby fighter aerodrome of Hornchurch.

Frederick William Boxall, aged 21, was killed when his Gloucester Gauntlet plummeted into the corner of the eastern boundary, close to the A12 road. He had been performing acrobatics over the area at an estimated height of about two thousand feet, when, without any warning, part of the top starboard wing cracked and broke away, thus causing the the aircraft to spiral towards the ground in an uncontrollable spin.

One of the eye witnesses to the incident was Mr Claude Oscroft, who had been watching the acrobatics from outside the aerodrome workshops at the bottom of the field. When he saw the aircraft falling from the sky right above the workshops, he quickly alerted the men working inside, because he believed the 'plane would crash there.

Another two witnesses who had been watching from their back garden in Court Avenue were Mr Lawrence Wiles and his twelve year old daughter, Doris. They had watched it circling around a few times before it turned towards the aerodrome, when Mr Wiles noticed that the aircraft was beginning to fall; he started to run from home towards the aerodrome, closely followed by his daughter. By the time they had reached the boundary fence, a small group of people were already looking across the field and, as they made their way along the road to the bottom of the field, they began to see the full extent of the crash. The aircraft was partly buried nose down in the ground and a few yards from the wreckage was a tarpaulin covering what Mr Wiles assumed to be the pilot's body. It was miraculous how Sergeant Boxall had managed to guide his stricken aircraft away from all the buildings on the aerodrome and from the surrounding houses, thus averting possibly more fatalities.

It was always believed that the Mercury engine from the aircraft was not recovered from the site, but I am able to confirm that, after a weekend's painstakingly gridding out the crash area and searching with deep-seeking metal detectors, no sign of the engine was found, and, although small fragments of aluminium were dug up, these could easily have come from any aircraft on the site, as none had any distinguishing marks. It is also likely that some of the pieces had come from the nearby workshops, as most aerodromes used to put rubbish into pits somewhere on the site.

Although no trace of Sergeant Boxall's aircraft was found, other items that did come to light were relics from Edward Hillman's day, such as a fork and spoon from the restaurant, that had been made by Mappin & Webb and have been dated circa 1930; various pieces of burnt aluminium from the hanger that burned down in 1940; an aircraft carburetor; and many coins of the time.

No official answers have yet been found in any Air Ministry or Public Record archives as to the explanation for the crash. Searches for these findings will continue, as they would be welcomed by 'Billy's' family, who have never been told what really happened. One theory is that an RAF court-martial took place, possibly for one of the ground crew, which would explain why no paperwork appertaining to the incident can be traced. The records of such trials are kept secret for one hundred years, which means that they should be released to public gaze sometime in 2037.

It is inevitable that, after so many months of intensive investigation into this tragic incident, I feel that I have come to know Sergeant Boxall on a very personal level. What started out as just another piece of research into an unknown airman's fatal accident in a Gloucester Gauntlet turned into a search for more information on a long-lost friend. It is only when you really start digging deep into a personal story like Billy's that one starts to fell a real sadness at the terrible loss of life of one so young. There is no doubt in my mind that this brave young pilot struggled not only with his stricken aircraft on that day, but also with his own thoughts – should he he jump and save himself without care for innocent bystanders, or should he try to keep his aircraft away from surrounding buildings and avert the possibility of even greater loss of life. The decision he made in itself must tell you something of the man's strong character, especially if his age is considered and that he had only gained his RAF wings some thirteen months previously.

Date and Hour	Aeroplane Type and No.	Pilot	Passenger(s)	Time	Height	Course	REMARKS
21.11.35	2Y	Ellison	Self.	60	4,000	Local	Steep Turns. Spinning Climbing turns. Side-slipping.
21.11.35	2Y	Self.	Solo.	15	700	Local	Taking off into wind, Landing & judging distance
22.11.35	2Y	Self.	Solo	35	800	Local	Taking off into wind. Landing & judging distance
22.11.35	2Y	Ellison	Self.	35	2,000	Local	Gliding turns. Sideslipping.
22.11.35	2Y	Self.	Solo	35	700	Local	Taking off into wind. Landing & judging distance.
23.11.35	2Y	Self.	Solo	75	4,000	Local	Spinning. Turns, Sideslips. Landings.
23.11.35	2Y	Self.	Solo	45	11,000	Local.	Height test.
23.11.35	2Y	Ellison	Self.	35	4,000	Local	Steep turns without engine
23.11.35.	2Y	Self.	Solo.	25	3,000	Local.	Turns, spins & sideslips

A page from William Boxall's training log

Reading through some of his flying and training log records, it would seem that Billy could have progressed into a much finer pilot than he already was, perhaps even becoming a fighter Ace during the Battle of Britain had fate not cruelly intervened.

Gloucester Gauntlet Interceptor Fighters

AIR CADETS

With the rumblings of war throughout Europe, Britain now saw a need to strengthen its defences and one idea put forward was to enlist the help of the young people and form them into a trained defence unit. This developed into the Air Defence Cadet Corps (ADCC), later known as the Air Training Corps (ATC).

By the start of March, 1938, Romford had seen the formation of the first Romford Air Patrol, who met in a disused Romford store during the week, but were allowed on a real aerodrome at weekends. Eric Coates's *London Bridge* would be blasted out over the public address system, with the Cadets having to march up and down to it. They also had use of an old fuselage from a two seater Bulldog to train with, while the wings of the Bulldog were stored in nearby hangers.

There was also a great deal of activity from the Civil Air Guard, who were very distinctively dressed in their green overalls. There were also occasional visits from the Auxiliary Air Force (AAF) and the Royal Air Force Volunteer Reserve (RAFVR). Until almost the outbreak of war aircraft would make flying visits to the cadets; on one particular flypast a Hawker Hurricane of 151 Squadron from North Weald made a couple of low level sweeps across the aerodrome and this was, for many of the amazed onlookers, their first view of the new look monoplane fighter – it would certainly not be their last such sighting!

DH Fox Moth, G-ABVI, belonging to the Romford Flying Club, parked at Maylands on 18th April, 1938

Some of the young men from the Air Defence Cadet Corps in front of aircraft owned by the Romford Flying Club

THE LAST DAYS OF PEACE

In the lead-up to the Second World War there were still many pleasureable hours of flying to be had at Maylands while the Romford Flying Club was in residence. This was now more in evidence as many ordinary people were able to pay a small fee and take over the aircraft controls – many of them gaining their pilot's licence. 1939 was a record year for the Flying Club with no fewer than eight first time solos and five 'A' class licences being secured by members attached to the Civil Air Guard, the National Women's Air Reserve and the Flying Club itself. The first solos went to Messrs Mantle, Felt, Bewster, King, Dolby, Armour, Abthorpe and Smith, with the 'A' licences being awarded to Messrs Armour, Lane, Parker, Dolby and Hurstwayte.

From the *Romford Times*, 20th July, 1938

FLYING GIRLS IN FUN FAIR

The 'flying girls' of the National Women's Air Reserve are holding a fun fair at Maylands aerodrome on Saturday, in aid of the funds of the reserve. There will be the usual attractions of the fair, including a treasure hunt competition, ankle judging, and an open darts competition. In the evening there will be dancing in the open air and a cabaret. Admission to the aerodrome will be sixpence.

During the 1930s Mr V C Hall's Airport Engineering Company was located in one of the hanger workshops at the bottom of the field. They worked on many of the aircraft flying in and out of Maylands, offering minor repair work of a full overnight service.

The company left the site just prior to the outbreak of war, moving into new premises at Harold Court Road, about a quarter of a mile from the aerodrome. As their headed notepaper demonstrates they became one of the many contractors carrying out work for the War Office; they were making parts for the Air Ministry and also working on the anti-aircraft guns at Warley Barracks in Brentwood. Today this small business still trades under the same name, although the company is no longer owned by the Hall family, but it is nice to recognise a link with Mayland's past.

THE LAST DAYS

After twelve short years the final curtain was to fall on the one-time prosperous aerodrome at Maylands when it was unceremoniously burnt to the ground on the night of 6th February, 1940. It happened during an alleged German bombing raid over the Romford area and all the buildings and the aircraft belonging to the Romford Flying Club were destroyed.

DH 83 Fox Moth 'Chris', formerly owned by Hillman's Airways,
was destroyed in the fire of 6th February, 1940

From the *Romford Recorder* 9th February, 1940

FIRE DESTROYS EIGHT 'PLANES
AERODROME HANGAR ABLAZE
THREE BRIGADES CALLED
Members of three fire brigades – Romford, Hornchurch and Brentwood – were engaged for three hours on a fire on Tuesday night which destroyed eight civil aircraft housed in a large hangar at the Maylands Aerodrome, Harold Park, occupied by the Romford Flying Club.

The three brigades were called because the aerodrome is on the extreme edge of the boundary of each brigade's area. Auxiliary Fire Service units from each brigade also took part. Owing to the weather conditions, an

AFS car and trailer pump ran off the road and stopped in a ditch while on its way to the fire.

The firemen were aided in their efforts by an adequate supply of water from a stream running along the edge of the aerodrome and they succeeded in preventing the flames spreading to a storeroom and a room used for flying instruction in connection with the Civil Air Guard and the Air Cadets.

Since the outbreak of war both these organisations had ceased and the aerodrome had been closed.

In addition to the destruction of the hangar, an office was partially burned. The roof of the hangar fell in and the walls collapsed.

The fire made a bright red glare, and a small crowd of people was attracted to the spot, and police were engaged in keeping civilians away from the aerodrome while the hangar was burning.

Very soon after the outbreak the hangar and its contents was a smouldering mass of twisted black metal, and only the metal framework of the aeroplanes remained.

The case of the fire is being investigated, but the police do not attach any importance to the suggestion that it was the result of sabotage or any I R A activities.

SECOND CALL

While the Romford brigade was at the aerodrome a call was received to a house in Sheila Close, Collier Row, occupied by Mr W Jordan, where a chimney fire occurred. The flames were quickly extinguished before any serious damage was done.

Other theories say that the aerodrome was deliberately set alight for insurance purposes and even that the IRA had sabotaged it, mistaking it for RAF Hornchurch. We will probably never know what really happened that night, but the aerodrome was never to re-open to any form of flying again, although 18th October, 1940, would see one of the last aircraft to land at Maylands in the form of Hurricane P5206 flown by French pilot, Sergeant Buoquillard of 249 Squadron, North Weald. It had been low on fuel and had to make an emergency crash landing; both the pilot and his 'plane were slightly shaken, but unscathed.

Sergeant Buoquillard, his Hurricane, and a policeman

Mrs Beatrice May Ewington arriving (in rather better order) at Alton Park, Clacton, aerodrome in 1933 after a 30 minute flight from Maylands on Hillman Airway's DH Fox Moth G-ABVK 'Doreen'

Romford (Maylands)

DT/TM-3/Great Britain, Romford (Maylands)/Neg No. 85

N51 E-0

Lange(ostw.Greenw): 0 °15'45", Breite·51°36'30"

Messung-10°35(Mitte 1938)

Maßstab etwa 1 : 10000 (1 cm = 100 m)

A German aerial photograph of Maylands on 24th May, 1939

THE PRESENT

Today, Maylands still enjoys a great success as a private golf club over sixty years after its opening and you will find, nestling in one corner of the splendid clubroom, the visitors' board, preserving the many famous names from the past, that have attended functions there.

And what of the former aerodrome? It now stands quiet and abandoned almost totally forgotten, but for any aviation archaeologists there are some tell-tale signs if you look closely enough and you are able to find some of its original hangar foundations and concrete bases, along with a great expanse of boarding apron from which many passengers departed on their adventure with flight. In places the site is now rather overgrown and moss covered, but these historic relics are still worth looking out for should you be invited to look around the site.

Fallow deer now roam freely across the ground that once heard the sound of roaring aircraft engines. Even though this small Essex aerodrome has now disappeared into the depths of aviation history it will not be totally forgotten, nor should the important role that Edward Hillman played in its shaping, for without this 1930s entrepreneur we may not have seen the likes of Freddie Laker during the 70s or Richard Branson in today's aviation business world.

It is a sad fact that only one example from each of Edward Hillman's vast fleet of aircraft and buses still survives. The Historic Commercial Vehicle Society now own the only known Gilford bus, JD 1981, to have operated for the company, but this is at the present in a very poor state of repair as it had been stored in the open air for many years prior to Michael Banfield buying it on behalf of the Society. It is hoped that it will eventually be restored to something like its former condition.

That is exactly what has happened to the last Hillman's Airways DH 89 Dragon Rapide, G-ADAH. This aircraft is now owned by the Aeroplane Collection and went through an extensive four year restoration programme. It is now on static display in the Manchester Museum of Science and Industry. The aircraft is in the livery of Allied Airways (Gandar Dower Ltd), the company to whom it was sold after leaving Hillman's fleet.

EDWARD HILLMAN

Edward Hillman had always chosen to try to live locally to his business ventures and so he had purchased a house at 145 Hare Street (now known as Main Road). The house was named Gilford Lodge, because of Hillman's long association with the Gilford Motor Company.

It is said that he had the front hedges cut into the shapes of some of his aircraft and that in the centre of the front garden stood a large metallic sphere which sat astride an obelisk. The house still exists, and I have had the privilege of visiting it, thanks to its present owner, although my original expectations of what the house would be like were. rather shattered when I first saw it, as I had always imagined it to be a far grander place with large wrought iron gates leading down a long driveway, but in reality the house is no different to any of its neighbours.

EXHIBITIONS

While writing this book, I have had the great pleasure of staging two very successful exhibitions, dedicated to 'The Maylands Aerodrome Story'. The first took place. in May 1999 and was held over a three week period at Harold Wood Library, just a short distance away from the site. This was the first time that an exhibition of photographs, written text and artefacts covering the aerodrome had been assembled, and it was received well by the many local people who saw it,

The second exhibition came about when I asked Mr Philip Taylor, the present owner of the Maylands Golf Club. how he felt about bringing back part of the site's history for a one-off exhibition. He was only too happy to allow me to do so and suggested that I use part of the splendid clubhouse for the display, which took place on 1st and 2nd April, 2000. Two very specially invited guests who attended were Mr Charles Whitby, the half-brother of Frederick William Boxall, the RAF pilot tragically killed there in 1937, and his wife. They drove from their London home to see the exhibition and visit the crash site.

This newspaper article comes from the *Yellow Advertiser*, May 1999.

AERODROME DISPLAY TAKES OFF AT LIBRARY

A colourful tale of the old Maylands aerodrome is to take place at Harold Wood Library, highlighting its rise to prominence with the 1930s playboys until its demise in early 1940.

In the first ever exhibition dedicated to the aerodrome photographs, text and artefacts have all been brought together, they will be on show from May 10th until May 28th. Mr Anthony Philpot, the organiser, said the exhibition will help schoolchildren learn about their area and will bring back fond memories for those who can remember the aerodrome. At the heart of the story is the larger-than-life entrepreneur, Edward Hillman, who developed passenger flights down to the coast and also over to Paris, Ostend, La Bourget. Other highlights of the exhibition include the account of an RAF pilot who tragically crashed at Maylands in 1937, and the story surrounding the site's destruction.

The following press release was issued on the 7th April 2000.

AERODROME'S HISTORY FINALLY COMES HOME

Back in 1928, after Mr A H Matthews, began using part of the Maylands farm as a small private landing strip, who could of realised that just three years later when Mr Edward Hillman, a local bus operator became the new licensee, that things would really start to take off?

Hillman's Airways soon opened up many regular passenger routes to most parts of the Essex countryside, and then even on as far as Paris.

But after a short time it soon became clear that Hillman's needed to expand its operations and by June of 1934 they departed to nearby Stapleford Tawney. By 1936 part of the aerodrome had been sold off to a consortium for a proposed golf course. The aerodrome would continue to operate for a further four years until it was totally destroyed by fire on the night of 6th February, 1940.

Now, some seventy-two years later the aerodrome's history has been rekindled for an exhibition staged in the splendid clubhouse of the Maylands Golf Club. The display, which took place over the weekend of 1st-2nd April, was staged by the Essex Airfields Historical Group, and is the culmination of three years hard work by the group's founder, Mr Anthony Philpot.

The highlight of the weekend's proccedings was undoubtedly the visit of Mr Charles Whitby, who is the step-brother of the late Sergeant F W Boxall, the young RAF pilot of 65 (F) Squadron who was based at the nearby fighter station at Hornchurch, who was tragically killed in May 1937 when his Gloster Gauntlet aircraft crashed on the aerodrome.

HILLMAN'S AIRWAYS PILOTS

Some of the men and women employed by Edward Hillman at both Maylands and Stapleford Tawney were either ex-Royal Flying Corps or Royal Air Force pilots. When the conflicts of the Second World War started, many of them would rejoin the services becoming ferry pilots; the most famous of these was Miss Amy Johnson who was unfortunately lost somewhere over the Thames Estuary in 1941, while flying for the Air Transport Auxiliary.

Harold 'Timber' Woods. Walter Robert Bannister.
John Lock. John Oliver. Leonard Van Oppen.
H E Flowerday. R D Crundall. T W 'Sammy' Moreton.
John Kirton. Amy Johnson.
W Anderson. Nigel Pelly. 'Flip' Fleming.
H W Easdon. Pauline Gower.

Amy Johnson (1903-41) made her name by flying solo to Australia in 1930:
She then made a record flights to Tokyo in 1931, South Africa in 1932, Karachi
(with James Alan Mollison, whom she married in 1932) in 1934
and Cape and back, 1936.
She was made a C B E in 1930

HILLMAN'S AIRWAYS LIMITED 1931 - 1935 AIRCRAFT FLEET LIST.

D.H. 60m Moth G-ABCW   c/n* 1552   unit no.3   Sold in India as VT-AEC April 1933

D.H. 60 GIII Moth G-ACGX   c/n 5029   To Cinema Press Ltd, Croydon June 1936

D.H. 80A Puss Moth G-ABSB   c/n 2213   unit no.1 'Sonny'   sold 1933

D.H. 80A Puss Moth G-ABSO   c/n 2217   unit no.2 'Babs'   withdrawn and sold July 1936

D.H. 80A Puss Moth G-ABVX   c/n 2228   unit no.4 'Gilford'   sold November 1935

D.H. 83 Fox Moth G-ABVI   c/n 4004   unit no.5 'Chris'   to Essex Aero Ltd, Maylands, July 1936   (Burnt out in the hanger fire on 6th February 1940)

D.H. 83 Fox Moth G-ABVJ   c/n 4006   To Eastern Air Transport Ltd, Skegness, July 1933

D.H. 83 Fox Moth G-ABVK   c/n 4005   unit no.6 'Doreen' to British Airways Ltd, Stapleford, January 1936

D.H. 84 Dragon I G-ACAN   c/n 6000   unit no.7 'Maylands' to Aberdeen Airways, Dyce, September 1934

D.H. 84 Dragon I G-ACAO   c/n 6001   unit no.8 'Goodmayes' to Lady Apsley, Whitchurch, October 1935

D.H. 84 Dragon I G-ACAP   c/n 6002   unit no.9 'Romford' to Commercial Air Hire Ltd, Croydon, Feburary 1936

D.H. 84 Dragon 1 G-ACBW   c/n 6009   'Gidea Park' to Provincial Airways Ltd, Croydon, July 1934

D.H. 84 Dragon I G-ACEU   c/n 6022 unit no.11 'Brentwood' to Airwork Ltd, Heston, January 1936

D.H. 84 Dragon I G-ACEV   c/n 6023   unit no.12 'Ilford' to Airwork Ltd, Heston, December 1935

D.H. 89 Dragon Rapide G-ACPM   c/n 6251   Lost four miles off Folkestone, 2nd October 1934

D.H. 89 Dragon Rapide G-ACPN   c/n 6252   Sold Spain, August 1936

D.H. 89 Dragon Rapide G-ACPO   c/n 6253   Sold Australia, VH-UBN, August 1936

D H. 89 Dragon Rapide G-ADDF   c/n 6284   Northern & Scottish Airways, Ltd.,
August 1936

D.H.86 Express G-ADEA   c/n 2323   'Drake' to British Airways December, 1935

D.H. 86 Express G-ADEB   c/n 2324   British Airways Ltd December, 1935

D.H. 86 Express G-ADEC   c/n 2325   British Airways, Ltd December, 1935

*Aircraft Code Number issued by the Civil Aviation Authority

The entire fleet for Hillman's Airways

supplied by

BRIAN LEWIS AND COMPANY LIMITED

THE WORLD'S

GREATEST

AIRCRAFT

DISTRIBUTORS

Brian Lewis & Co. Ltd.

30, CONDUIT STREET, LONDON, W.1

DE HAVILAND DISTRIBUTORS.

All types of Aircraft introduced to interested clients.

**AERODROMES: HESTON (London)   HOUTON
LIVERPOOL and IPSWICH**

ACKNOWLEDGEMENTS

Mr Peter Baines, Rolls Royce Enthusiasts' Club; London Transport Museum; Mr Edward Mann, ex-Hillman employee; Mr Jim Nightingale, Stapleford Aerodrome; Mr Michael Banfield, Historical Commercial Vehicle Society; British Airways Archives and Museum Collection; Rod & Derrick Aspinall, Airscene Museum; Mr Charles Whitby; Castle Point Transport Museum Society; R.A.F. Hendon Museum, air historical branch; Public Record Office; The Aeroplane Collection Ltd; Aeroplane Monthly; Essex Record Office; National Museums of Scotland; Corporation of London Record Office; Civil Aviation Authority; London Borough of Havering Library Services; Postal History Society; Thanet District Council; Patent Office; R.A.F. Manston History Club; Mr Philip Taylor, Mayland Golf Club; Manchester Museum of Science and Industry; Essex County Libraries; Mr Sid Bowen (secretary) 600 City of London Squadron Association; British Library; British Aerophilatelic Federation; Mr Lawrence Wiles; Mr Ron Shipton, R.A.F. Hornchurch Association; Science Museum Library;   Mr J T Williams Collection; Mr John Nicholls; Airfield Research Group; Mr Reg Taylor, Hillman collector; Mr John Hamlin; The PSV Circle; Chelmsford Museum Service; Mr Brian Evans; Mr Peter Snell, Essex Bus Enthusiasts' Group; Mr Alan Osborne; South Ealing Cemeteries Department; Mr Stephen Sutton, North Weald Airfield Museum; Mr John Bush, Hillman collector; Mr A Tilbrook, *Essex Countryside* magazine; Mr M. Ewington; Mrs E L Butler; Mr D R Brittain; Mrs J B Brett; Mr F Adcock; Mr M D Wright; Mr F B Green; Mr D Jones, Gilford Motor Company Research; Mr E Green, Group Archivist of HSBC; Mr P Watt; Mrs A Rodway, Clacton Library; Mr D Potter, aviation philatelic collector; Mr C Hawkins; Mr L Hall, former owner of Airport Engineering; *Flypast* magazine; Mr A Tomlin; Mr K Tomlin; Alacrity printers & stationers; Mr R Morris; Mrs D Lobley; Mr N Doyle; Mr T Dendy; Mrs Knight; Mr C Stewart.

During my time compiling this book, it has been a great pleasure for me to meet, talk to and correspond with the many individuals, companies and organisations who have kindly allowed me access to their personal memories, private papers, photographs and historical documents. It is without doubt their most invaluable help during this project, that has enabled me to put together the complete history of Maylands Aerodrome.

De Havilland 86
G-ADEB
Photographed at
Stapleford

All the following books are recommended as background reading for anyone interested in Maylands or Stapleford Tawney aerodromes, and the life of Mr Edward Hillman.

Action Stations 8 Military airfields of Greater London - Bruce Barrymore Halpenny
The Airmails of the British Isles - H. S. Redgrove
Battle of Britain Then and Now - Winstone Ramsey
The History of British bus services – John Hibbs
Clacton on Sea, a pictorial history - Norman Jacobs
'First Things First': RFC Suttons Farm and RAF Hornchurch, 1915-1962 - Eric Smith
Gentlemen in Blue - Hans Onderwater
Havering Village to Harold Wood - Chris Saltmarsh & Norma Jennings
London's Buses Volume 2 - Ken Blacker, Ron Lunn, Reg Westgate
No Highway - Nevil Shute
Ominous Skies 1935 - 1939 - Harold Penrose
Peaceful Fields - John F. Hamlin
Preserved Aircraft - Keith Johnson
Railway Air Services - John Stroud
Romford, Collier Row, Gidea Park - Brian Evans
Sky Fever - Autobiography of Sir Geoffrey De Havilland
Slide Rule - Nevil Shute
The Story of a Pioneer in Civil Transport - Michael Conn

Anyone wishing to obtain further information on Edward Hillman or his company, Hillman Saloon Coaches and Airways Limited, should send a S. A. E. to The Maylands Aerodrome Research Society, c/o 88 Kempton Avenue, Hornchurch, Essex, RM12 6EB.

This classic Gilford JD 1981, formerly of Hillman's fleet, was photographed in the 1950s in this derelict condition

'FIRST THINGS FIRST'

RAF Hornchurch and RFC Suttons Farm

1915 - 1962

Eric Smith

The first air-ship to be destroyed over England
was shot down by an airman flying from
RFC Suttons Farm,
but the glory days of the station were as
RAF Hornchurch,
when it bore the brunt of the
Battle of Britain in 1940.
Later it combatted the flying bomb menace
and, later still, became a training ground
for aircrew personnel.
Many famous names in aviation flew
from Hornchurch
and their triumphs and tragedies are here recorded

£14.95

Ian Henry Publications, Ltd.
20 Park Drive, Romford, Essex RM1 4LH